William Wallace

*A Captivating Guide to a Freedom Fighter
and Martyr Who Impacted Scottish History
and Scotland's Independence from England*

Free Bonus from Captivating History
(Available for a Limited time)

Hi History Lovers!

Now you have a chance to join our exclusive history list so you can get your first history ebook for free as well as discounts and a potential to get more history books for free! Simply visit the link below to join.

Captivatinghistory.com/ebook

Also, make sure to follow us on:

Twitter: @Captivhistory

Facebook: Captivating History:@captivatinghistory

Contents

Introduction

Sir William Wallace (c. 1270 – 1305) was – and is – a Scottish national icon of the highest order.[i] Born as the landless younger son of a minor nobleman (Sir Malcolm Wallace), his startling rise to become a military and historical legend, an exemplary patriot, and a national hero is an embodiment of the underdog narrative that many people identify with in film and real life. Wallace earned a place in history for his successful efforts in leading the Scottish resistance forces who had been rallying against English rule since Scotland was conquered in 1296.

On the 11th of September, 1297, Wallace achieved a monumental victory at the Battle of Stirling Bridge.[ii] Wallace and his men were severely outnumbered, but his English enemies had to cross a narrow bridge to attack them. His men slaughtered them as they crossed the river, leaving five thousand English soldiers dead on the field. Wallace thus captured Stirling Castle and momentarily freed Scotland of its occupying forces. Wallace was then knighted as "Commander of the Army of the Kingdom of Scotland."

In a hierarchy-obsessed medieval period, Wallace's rise from a mere knight to the Guardian of Scotland was unthinkable. His military prowess had allowed him to exert power over Scottish nobles, causing many of them to resent his influence. He sent letters to

Europe, proclaiming Scotland's renewed independence from English rule. He ordered his troops to attack England's northern territories (the counties of Northumberland and Cumberland).

Wallace's legendary status had been preserved in his home country of Scotland ever since fifteenth-century Scottish royal court poet Harry the Minstrel (or "Blind Harry"[iii]) wrote *The Actes and Deidis of the Illustre and Vallyeant Campioun Schir William Wallace* (*Acts and Deeds of the Illustrious and Valiant Champion Sir William Wallace*, a.k.a. *The Wallace*). Published nearly 200 years after his death, this "romantic biographical" poem eventually became the second most popular book in Scotland after the Bible – a position that it has retained for centuries.[iv]

Most people outside of Scotland probably became acquainted with Mel Gibson's 1995 film, *Braveheart*[v] (which he directed and starred in). The movie (which was made by Hollywood, with an American/Australian actor cast in the leading role) went on to gross $210.4 million worldwide. It also garnered critical acclaim. It was nominated for ten Academy Awards at the 68th Academy Awards. It went home with five Oscars at the end of that night: Best Picture, Best Director, Best Cinematography, Best Makeup, and Best Sound Editing. It catalyzed massive worldwide interest in Scotland and Scottish history – a definite win for Scottish tourism.

The film's voiceover acknowledges the fact that English historians have described Wallace as a traitor, an outlaw, a murderer, and a man who committed many atrocities. "Historians from England will say I am a liar, but history is written by those who have hanged heroes." Ironically, however, Scottish historians will also concede that the movie is riddled with glaring historical inaccuracies (Gibson himself has admitted that the film is a "historical fantasy").[vi] These inaccuracies go beyond the general gap between the popular tales about Wallace and the concrete historical records. The film includes wild narrative inventions like the "ius primae noctis" policy (where the invading English nobles give themselves the legal right to interrupt Scottish weddings and replace the groom during the bride's wedding night), blue face paint, and an affair with Princess Isabella of France (who was a child at that time, and only married the Prince of Wales three years after Wallace died).[vii]

The film also glosses over the bloody grittiness of Wallace's tragic death.[viii] King Edward I had been campaigning in France during Wallace's reign.[ix] He returned to England in March 1298, and then invaded Scotland on July 3. Wallace was ultimately unable to repeat his military success at the Battle of Falkirk,[x] which took place on 22 July 1298. The English nobility had been deeply dissatisfied with Edward I's rule during the nation's wars with France and Scotland. England's humiliating defeat at the hands of the Scots at Stirling Bridge nevertheless united them against Wallace. Their forces included the deadly and relatively sophisticated Welsh archers, who had a greater firing range with their longbows than their Scottish opponents who used slingshots. During medieval warfare, when most of the fighting was done up close, the use of the longbow was revolutionary.

The defeat destroyed Wallace's reputation as a military icon. He resigned from his position as Guardian of Scotland and then disappeared for over four years. There is some evidence that he went to France in 1299 and subsequently became a guerrilla leader. By 1304, most of the Scottish nobles had resigned themselves to accept King Edward I's rule. The English, however, were determined to capture Wallace and force him to pay for his defiance, and his refusal to submit amounted to a death sentence.

On August 5, 1305, Wallace was arrested in the vicinity of Glasgow. At London, he was found guilty of treason and for the atrocities against English civilians during the war. Wallace retorted that he had never been a subject of the English king. In the movie, Gibson's Wallace is simply hanged after the verdict was delivered. The real Wallace, however, was subjected to the five-stage punishment that was administered to many famous traitors.[xi] Before he was hanged, he was stripped naked and dragged through London by a rope tied to the heels of a horse. He was then hanged (strangled, but released before dying), disemboweled, castrated, beheaded, and then quartered. His head was preserved and placed on a pike on the London Bridge. The four quarters of his body were displayed individually in Perth, Stirling, Berwick, and Newcastle.

After Wallace's grisly execution, it appeared that the Scottish revolt had also been quelled. The next year, however, Robert the Bruce[xii] – who replaced Wallace alongside John Comyn as joint guardians of Scotland [xiii] – raised another rebellion that finally won Scotland's independence and ended the nation's First War of Independence. Wallace's death had certainly not been in vain; his fiercely defiant spirit lives on in his countrymen and women. Centuries later, the sacrifices he made for Scottish freedom continue to resonate, while historians painstakingly scrutinize the folktale and legends to locate the man behind the myth.

Chapter 1 – Mysterious Origins

The gory conditions of Wallace's death are well documented, but there is insufficient evidence to conclusively settle the case for his origins. His exact year of birth is unknown. Records have been as varied as 1260 and 1278, but 1270 serves as the most probable year. His location of birth has also been contested. Since his name was styled 'of Ellerslie' due to the land that was owned by his father, Sir Malcolm Wallace (who was styled 'of Auchenbothie and Ellerslie'), many assumed that he was born in the Renfrewshire town of Elderslie.[xiv] The town still proclaims itself to be birthplace of Scotland's national hero. Its attractions include a small castellated house that is deemed to be his birthplace, an old yew tree known as Wallace's Yew, Wallace's Tavern, and a distinctive monument that was erected in 1970.

Much of the confusion about Wallace's origins comes from the epic poem *The Wallace*,[xv] written by fifteenth-century court poet Blind Harry (c. 1440 – 1492). Blind Harry claimed to have based his poem on a prose manuscript that was compiled by John Blair. Blair had been Wallace's friend in school, and then his chaplain. This manuscript has never been found (some doubt it ever existed), so there is no way of proving how faithfully or unfaithfully Blind Harry adhered to it. After all, Blind Harry was probably not born blind or as uneducated as he presented himself to be. He probably also drew from the many myths, anecdotes, and folktales about Wallace that circulated during his time. In any case, historians have already located many historical errors in the text.

Historian James Mackay argues that Wallace had actually been born in the lesser-known county of Ayrshire, within the district of Kyle.[xvi] Ellerslie, or Elderslie, are different variants of the same name, which has been used to refer to Ayrshire and Renfrewshire in maps and documents (Ayrshire is confusingly also known as Elderslie today). Ellerslie, Ayrshire, had been a simple hamlet that revolved around coal mining and brickworks until the Second World War. Little of it remains today.

Where the Wallaces came from is also a matter of debate. The medieval names Walays, Waleys, or Wallensis refer to a Welshman within the English languages spoken by the Englishmen and Scotsmen of the time. It is thus certainly possible that the Wallaces in the area were medieval immigrants from Wales (an origin story that Blind Harry perpetuated). James Mackay, however, notes that the surviving land titles and buildings cannot conclusively connect William Wallace to the more eminent Wallaces that could trace back their ancestral roots to Wales. There are also contradictory speculations that suggest Wallace might have Anglo-Danish ancestry instead.

What historians can agree on, however, is the fact that Wallace was born in Scotland in 1270, when it was wealthy and peaceful. King Alexander III had been ruling since 1249; political stability had ushered in an era of prosperity and harmony. [xvii] This was a country adorned with majestic cathedrals, magnificent abbeys, and grand monasteries. There were also hundreds of castles that were home to the aristocrats, barons, and knights, and stately homes that belonged to the landed classes. By this time, the Scots had been under the rule of only one monarch for nearly four generations. Many of them were more in touch with royals than a national identity. Much of the economic and political activity of the era revolved around Berwick, which was strategically placed at the mouth of the River Tweed. At its port, Scottish merchants traded with the Low Countries, northern Germany, and Scandinavia. The country's capital, Edinburgh, was similar in size to Berwick. There were nearly half a million people in Scotland at the time, while there were approximately 2 million in England. The relationship between the two countries was peaceful, but their border had never been definitively delineated. As a result, there had been many territorial disputes in the past.

Wallace was born into what would retrospectively be known as Scotland's "golden age." Scottish agriculture surpassed English agriculture during Alexander III's reign, with a dominant wool and cattle industry.[xviii] With low taxes, the people could enjoy the fruits of their labor by indulging in alcohol and a hearty diet. There were bridges and good roads that could speed up trade via wheeled carts, horseback, and wagons. Scotland was an exporter of fish, timber, wool, and hides. It looked toward northern Europe for international relations, instead of England.

As a young Wallace grew up with few worries, King Henry III of England died. He was replaced by his son, King Edward I, the man who would become his most powerful opponent. Both men's ambitions reflected the prosperity of their respective countries. Edward I was known as "Longshanks" for his tall stature, while Wallace would grow to a staggering height of two meters (six-foot-seven). When you consider the fact that the average height of an adult man at the time was only slightly over five feet, Wallace must have stood out easily after he hit puberty. Blind Harry's poem has been deemed to be accurate when it comes to describing his physicality.[xix] Wallace is noted for his large stature, broad shoulders, handsome face, great limbs, sturdy neck, wavy brown hair, piercing eyes, and overtly "manly make."

In an era where close combat (possibly with the help of a sword and dagger) was the order of the day during physical conflicts, Wallace's superhuman stature undeniably served him well. Without exemplary mental attributes, however, it is unlikely that he would have been able to attract and lead his followers toward historic glory.

Historians speculate that he received a secular and religious education from the monks in his area, as well as from his parents. Apart from learning to read and write, he would have also been equipped with horse riding and martial skills. He was trained in the art of fighting with the dirk (a long thrusting dagger) and the claymore (a tall two-handed sword). A claymore was nearly six feet in length, taller than most men living at the time. When a figure as tall and strong as Wallace whirled it into an opponent, it was enough to slash through the armor of the time.

Wallace was probably between eleven to thirteen years old when Edward I finished his conquest of Wales (in 1283, after six years). In 1285, he traveled to Paris to pay homage to its new King, Philip the Fair.[xx] He would remain there for three years, apparently secure that England and Wales were firmly under control. Instead, many of his ministers and judges turned to greater heights of corruption while he was away. After returning in 1289, he decided to expel all Jews from his kingdom, using them as a scapegoat for the political chaos and economic strife at the time. He then turned his ambitious gaze toward Scotland.

Chapter 2 – Coming of Age in Crisis

When Wallace was approximately fourteen years old, Scotland was struck with a national crisis. On 18 March 1286, King Alexander attended a council in Edinburgh Castle. After that, he enjoyed fine wine with his barons over a good meal as a storm brewed outside. Instead of staying the night at the Castle, he decided to return home to Kinghorn via horseback. Many surmised that he was eager to return home to his young wife, Joleta of Dreux, France, who was half his age. He eventually became separated from his three esquires and two local guides in the darkness and howling winds. When they found him the next day, he was dead. His body was at the rocks at the foot of the cliffs.

The people had been expecting a male heir after the King's recent re-marriage (in 1285; after his first wife, Princess Margaret of England, died in 1275) and were stunned by the news of his death. This tragic news followed the death of Alexander's first two sons in 1281 and 1284. After two weeks of mourning, Alexander's granddaughter, Margaret of Norway,[xxi] was sworn in as the nation's sovereign lady. Her mother had died in childbirth, leaving her in the care of her father, King Eric II of Norway.[xxii] A provisional was established, with six Guardians of the Peace elected as regents. The Guardians were comprised of two earls, two barons, and two bishops.

Peace was maintained for the following three years. After that, powerful and competing factions began to appear on the national scene. The throne was empty, and there were powerful political players who aspired to occupy it. During this time, it is possible that Wallace and his father were called up for military service to defend the realm by the Guardians. The revolt was eventually resolved, but the authority of the Guardians had been called into question. As the composition of the Guardians changed with the death of two of the earls (one due to old age, the other murdered by his own family), Wallace's future was under discussion. As a landless younger son, Wallace was poised to pursue a religious career. His keen intelligence made this a good fit, and the parson of Dunipace – where Wallace was staying with an uncle – was known to be a wealthy and benevolent man. His uncle taught him moral maxims in Latin and exposed him to the eminent classical authors.

Plans were made for Margaret of Norway to marry Lord Edward, the five-year-old son of King Edward I when both were of age. The Treaty of Birgham was signed on 18 July 1920, uniting the two royal individuals while maintaining the separation of Scotland and England.[xxiii] Margaret was to be Scotland's 'true lady, queen and heir,' married to an English prince to preserve the peace between the two countries. Edward, on the other hand, intended to exert control over Scotland through matrimonial rights. When she died due to seasickness during the trip from Norway to Scotland, however, Scotland's hopes for independence were in peril. With her death, an ancient Scottish dynasty had arrived at a tragic end.

There were no less than thirteen candidates for the throne, each claiming a lineage from the Scottish royal family. If Margaret's mother had been alive, then her husband, Eirik II of Norway, would have a rightful claim to the throne. Some of the claims were based on being illegitimate offspring, which could not be granted serious consideration. Two primary candidates emerged from all this contestation: John de Balliol[xxiv] and Robert de Bruce.[xxv] Since each man was backed by armed forces, Scotland appeared to be on the brink of a civil war.

If England's King Edward had plans to take advantage of Scotland's leadership vacuum, he had to wait until the customary mourning period for his wife's passing was over. James Mackay has noted that Eleanor may have had a positive moral influence on her husband; her death thus freed him from any moral barriers toward violence and tyranny. While agreeing to advise the Scots on their succession crisis, he revealed to his privy council that he had plans to subdue Scotland as he had done with Wales.

Unfortunately for Wales and Scotland, Edward was one of England's most effective kings. The Scots would eventually refer to him as "Scottorum malleus" – the Hammer of the Scots – after he died in 1307. The reign of his father, Henry III,[xxvi] had been fraught with internal instability and military ineptitude. When he assumed the throne in 1272, he successfully negotiated peaceful relations between England's restless barons and united them under his rule. As a young man, he had proven himself on the battlefield as a soldier and military leader.

He was also a well-read monarch with an interest in new ideas that would reform the English government and administration. His means may have been highly unethical, but he was similarly successful when it came to raising money. He used his Parliament to maintain stability and collect large amounts of taxes from the population during his prosperous reign. In 1275, he imposed the popular Statute of Jewry, which imposed exorbitant levels of taxation on England's Jewish population. In 1290, all of England's Jews were expelled without their financial assets and property. He was thus financially well positioned to embark on an ambitious campaign of expansion.

The Guardians of Scotland's decision to invite Edward to adjudicate the competing claims to the Scottish throne eventually proved to be severely counterproductive. After years of fairly peaceful coexistence, they had wrongly assumed that English rule over Scotland was a matter of the past. King Willian I had acknowledged England's King Henry II as Scotland's feudal lord in 1174, but Scotland had retained a great degree of its independence throughout the thirteenth century. As such, they invited Edward – as an influential king and a notable expert on the legal aspects of statecraft – to be the judge on who was the rightful heir to the Scottish throne.

On 10 May 1291, King Edward proclaimed his rule over Scotland in front of an assembly of Scottish nobles and clergy. This justified his position as adjudicator in who was the next ruler of Scotland – and his position as Lord Paramount of Scotland. After the Scottish noblemen objected, he granted them three weeks to formulate a rebuttal. Meanwhile, he began marshaling his army to prepare for a possible military confrontation.

All the competitors for the throne eventually acknowledged Edward as Lord Paramount and consented to accepting his judgment. With most of them were in possession of large estates in England, the failure to do so would have almost certainly resulted in the forfeiture of these assets. Edward was careful enough to ensure that each competitor's acknowledgment was written down and graced with their official seal. After that, he ordered that every Scottish castle be surrendered to him temporarily until a successor had been chosen. Furthermore, all Scottish officials were to be replaced with Englishmen. All Scottish nobility, knights, freemen, and religious leaders were to swear their loyalty to Edward by 27 July or face severe penalties. Wallace's father, Sir Malcolm Wallace, refused to administer the oath and fled north with his eldest son when English officials were upon him.

Wallace was seventeen or eighteen at this time. He was sent to a nearby church school, which trained young men for a lifelong career as a priest. He met John Blair at this school. Blair would become a Benedictine monk and Wallace's comrade in arms, as well as the author of a Latin biography that Blind Harry would use as a reference for his epic poem.[xxvii] There was some resistance in

Dundee, but in general, the entire country was not particularly invested in resisting Edward's demands.

In December 1292, John Balliol was crowned King of Scotland:

> As it is admitted that the kingdom of Scotland is indivisible, and, as the king of England must judge of the rights of his subjects according to the laws and usages of the kingdoms over which he reigns; and as, by the laws and usages of England and Scotland in the succession to indivisible heritage, the more remote in degree of the first line of descent is preferable to the nearer in degree of the second line; therefore, it is decreed that John Balliol shall have seisin of the kingdom of Scotland.[xxviii]

He arguably had the better claim to the throne than Robert Bruce, being descended from an older royal sister. Bruce had argued that his claim was superior since he was the son of David I's great-granddaughter while John Balliol was the grandson of the great-grand-daughter (i.e. he was one less generation removed from the royal lineage). Balliol also owned land in the north of England, which made him likelier to acquiesce to Edward's mandates. Edward wasted no time in pressuring Balliol to accept his rule over Scotland and begin to assert his powers. When Balliol was crowned, Scotland was effectively under English occupation.

Scottish nobility may have conceded to the new status quo, but the common people did not simply accept the presence of the occupying English forces in their daily lives. They were fiercely proud of their national heritage and despised their elites for cowardly surrendering their authority to the English. Brawls and riots between the English soldiers and Scottish villagers and townspeople began to occur sporadically. One of these conflicts would claim the life of Sir Malcolm Wallace, leaving his son with a lifelong bitter resentment toward the English invaders.

Chapter 3 – Defiance and Compliance

Given the lack of concrete evidence, historians are unsure of the precise details of Wallace's evolution into a formidable guerrilla leader. According to Blind Harry, Wallace began to brazenly defy Edward's rule not long after his father's death. It thus appears that he began to take decisive actions to avenge his father and alleviate the oppression of his countrymen in 1291. The castle of Dundee, which had fallen under the possession of an English baron, served as the first stage for his defiance.

The baron, Brian Fitz-Alan of Bedale, was also a Guardian and Justice of Scotland. The castle was under the care of Selby, a constable that had inflicted much harm to the local community. His twenty-year-old son was known for causing mischief in the town on a daily basis with his friends. That December, the young Selby spotted Wallace's enormous frame and bright green clothes in the street. When Selby confronted him, he made fun of Wallace's appearance: "Thou Scot, abide; what devil clothed thee in so gay a garment? An Irish mantle were the right apparel for thy kind; a Scottish knife under thy belt to carry; rough shoes upon thy boorish feet."[xxix] He then demanded that Wallace surrender the dirk at his belt. Wallace responded by using it to stab him in the heart.

The crowd's interference allowed Wallace to wound Selby's comrades and make a quick exit. On his way to his uncle's townhouse, he met his uncle's housekeeper. After she learned of what he had done, he quickly had him wear one of her gowns and sat him down at her spindle. When the English soldiers arrived, they were fooled by the disguise. After failing to locate Wallace, they threatened to burn down the town unless the villagers surrendered him. Under the cover of night, Wallace escaped to Kilspindie via the alleys and back courts.

When the Dundee governor summoned all Scottish residents to appear at a court of enquiry, Wallace decided to leave the area. He disguised himself once again, this time as a pilgrim. He kept a short sword hidden under his gown. They pretended to be headed toward the shrine of Saint Margaret at Dunfermline (an English-born saint who had initiated the Anglicization of Scotland) whenever they were questioned by English patrolmen. By the time they arrived at Ellerslie, Wallace had been outlawed for murdering young Selby. His mother remained there while he headed to Reccarton to live with his uncle, Sir Richard Wallace.

On 23rd of February 1292, Wallace went on a fishing excursion with a servant, but without his weapons. There, five English soldiers demanded that he surrender his catch to them. Wallace decided to offer them half; the group's leader dismounted from his horse and seized the entirety of his catch. Wallace's refusal to submit eventually prompted the soldier to attack him with his sword. Wallace used his fishing-pole to defend himself and struck his opponent across the cheek. The blow was powerful enough to knock him off his feet and send his sword soaring through the air. Wallace seized the sword and killed his opponent by aiming at his neck. When the other four soldiers attacked, Wallace sliced through one of them to his collarbone and sliced off another's arm. The other two fled, leaving Wallace to finish off the one-armed soldier. Wallace took the soldier's gear and horses, and then escaped with his young page into the safety of the forest. The story of Wallace's exploits at

Irvine Water would survive to be his one of his earliest episodes of heroism.

While Wallace hid himself in the countryside, King John was negotiating the extent to which he could bring himself to oppose King Edward. Edward had warned that he would interfere in the country's affairs should John fail to "do justice" to his subjects and was likely indignant of the fact that he had to repeat his homage to Edward multiple times. In 1292, Edward flexed his influence by deciding a case at Newcastle. Roger Bartholomew had appealed to a higher authority after claiming that the Guardians of Scotland had treated him unfairly when presiding over his complex triple lawsuit. King John argued that Edward was violating the Treaty of Birgham, which mandated that all Scottish lawsuits be determined in Scotland. In response, Edward pronounced that he had the right to judge each and every Scottish case that was presented to him. He then coerced King John to acknowledge that the Treaty of Birgham was now void, and his actions were legally valid. Such maneuvers placed King John with little options but to comply, as the Scottish nobility – which had nurtured close ties with England for over two generations – were generally unwilling to support him in protest. This case established a precedent of appealing to the English courts when the Scottish courts made an unfavorable decision.

Edward maintained a position that he was only undermining King John's authority for the sake for maintaining law and order in Scotland, but it was clear to most observers that he was consciously undermining King John's position. This struggle for power swiftly eroded the relationship between the two leaders. In October 1293, Edward suffered the very same humiliations he had inflicted on King John. King Philip of France was his own feudal superior, and he decided to halt all trade between his country and England after a few English sailors went on a rampage at the La Rochelle port.

In response, Edward declared war against France in October 1294. Philip got Adolf of Germany to remain on neutral terms and secured the alliance of Florence of Holland and Eirik II of Norway; Edward was already dealing with a rebellion in Wales and needed all the assistance he could get. He thus ordered King John to marshal his forces and report to London by 1 September 1294. John seized the opportunity to rebel. On 22 October, he openly defied Edward by allying Scotland with Norway and France.

Edward prepared his armed forces and ships to prepare for a northern confrontation. He ordered King John to relinquish ownership of the castles and burghs of Berwick, Jedburgh, and Roxburgh and ordered English sheriffs to seize all of King John's assets in England. The first real confrontation between the Scots and English took place at the English town of Carlisle. Unable to penetrate its defenses, the Scots burned down the cottages and dwellings of its poorest denizens, which were outside its walls. They then pillaged, burned, and looted the villages, monasteries, and churches in the countryside before retreating past the Scottish border.

The English army – which then was comprised of three thousand foot soldiers and five thousand horsemen – retaliated by attacking Berwick, Scotland's largest city at the time. A few English merchants had been murdered at the port there five weeks earlier by a mob, which had then proceeded to loot their warehouses. Edward apparently intended to turn Berwick into an example. The townspeople were initially successful in defeating four of the five English ships that descended upon them. After that, however, they were in for a massacre. The town was ill-prepared for a military onslaught, but a local Flemish archer was successful in shooting down Richard of Cornwall, Edward's cousin. Edward ordered for the archer's base, the Red Hall, to be burned down to the ground. Over three days, thousands of townsmen, women, and children were raped and killed without mercy. Edward only ordered for his men to stop after witnessing a townswoman giving birth while one of his rampaging soldiers hacked her body to bits. By the time he called off the slaughter, between seventeen and twenty thousand Scottish townsfolk had died, nearly the entire population of Berwick at the time.

Edward had intended for the massacre to terrorize the entire population of Scotland. After generations of peaceful relations between the two countries, this bloody episode was intended to secure his authority over the country. Scottish historian and economist John Hill Burton noted that he had underestimated the common people's immense pride and honor, as well as their willingness to risk their lives in battle to defend it: "In his Norman sublimity, seeing only the persons worth seeing, the nobles, scarcely a step below himself in dignity and pretension, and of his own race, he had reckoned without that hitherto silent and inarticulate entity, the Scottish people."[xxx]

Instead of admitting defeat, the Scottish people united to support their king's defiance. On 5 April, King John formally renounced his allegiance to the English throne. Scottish bands attacked Redesdale, Tynedale, Cockermouth, and Hexham to avenge the atrocities at Berwick. Meanwhile, Edward set to work at rebuilding the very town that he had so thoroughly destroyed. After reinforcing its defenses, he designated Berwick as the administrative center of his new Scottish government in September 1296. Satisfied and smug with the knowledge that the Scottish elites would not unequivocally rally behind a king many perceived to be weak and ineffectual, he began planning his second attack.

He sent the English army northward, leading to confrontations with the Scottish army at Buchan. With his experienced horsemen, superior numbers, and veteran leaders, his army was able to secure a quick victory. 130 important Scottish knights were taken prisoner alongside several earls and influential magnates. After this, the spirit of Scottish resistance plummeted. The great Scottish castles – Roxburgh Castle, Edinburgh Castle, and Stirling Castle – were either conquered or abandoned. On July 2, King John formally surrendered his kingdom to England, while stating that his alliance with France was a mistake. Edward responded by subjecting him to ceremonial humiliations. Edward had the royal insignia ripped from John Balliol's surcoat, leaving him with the nickname Toom Tabard (empty coat) from then on. He was then shipped to England and placed under a comfortable house arrest.

With its king out of the way, Edward proceeded to further erode Scotland's national identity. He removed the Stone of Destiny (*Lia Fail*), the legendary basalt stone where every Celtic Scottish king had been crowned. It had been in the country since the sixth century after allegedly being brought over from the Holy Land under the care of Scota, the Pharaoh of Egypt's daughter, who lent the country her name. Edward arranged to have himself crowned on the stone, and then sent it to Westminster Abbey along with Scotland's crown jewels, which were only returned in 1996. Edward also shipped away three chests filled with royal records and other important archives. Whether they were lost, hidden, or destroyed, these precious documents were never recovered.

On 28 August 1296, Edward held his parliament at Berwick. The agenda was for the country's prominent bishops, earls, barons, abbots, and priors to pay homage to him and pledge their loyalties. He appointed a guardian of the land, a treasurer, and a chancellor. Edward did not establish himself as the King of Scotland; everyone paid homage to him as the King of England, Lord of Ireland, and Duke of Guyenne. Robert Bruce, Lord of Annandale, who had been allied with Edward throughout King John's rule, had been expecting to be named as John's successor. Edward was not interested in establishing another figurehead. When Bruce made his intentions known, Edward retorted with, "Have we nothing else to do but win you kingdoms?" [xxxi]Edward left the country eleven days after the ceremony, with the intention of focusing on his relations with France and other important matters. When winter came, a majority of the English soldiers there made the trip home. A few garrisons remained in all of Scotland's castles.

Chapter 4 – The Prophecy

Apart from the incident at Irvine Water, little concrete information about William Wallace's life during King John's rule is known. We know, however, that he came of age at a time when Scottish independence was a mirage. Everyone was more or less aware that their king had limited authority and influence over the matters in his own country. Important Scottish fortresses were in the hands of the English. English soldiers roamed the countryside, ready to exert their might against any common people who dared to depart from the expected humility and subservience. The usual processes of law and order were being eroded.

Naturally, William Wallace's exploits as an outlaw in the countryside throughout these years are not well documented. The myth that prevails is one that is similar to the legend of Robin Hood's brand of vigilante justice in the forests of Nottingham. Blind Harry describes him as a heroic defender of a fallen people; an embodiment of the people's desire to tip the scales of power in their favor:

> Although only eighteen years of age, he was seemly, robust and bold. He carried for weapons either a good sword or knife and with such he often had encounters with their English foes. When he found one without his fellow, such a one did no further harm to any Scot. To cut his throat or to stab him

suddenly he did not miss. Nor could anyone trace how he came by his death.[xxxii]

Wallace's indiscriminate savagery against the English may seem questionable and barbaric by today's standards, but they make sense when one considers the brutalities of the era. In the 1290s, the mortality rate was exceptionally high. Scottish people were routinely punished for various minor offences by flogging, mutilation, and public hanging. Without a just legal justice system in place, people often took the law into their own hands. English historians were quick to document and lament atrocities committed by Scottish robbers and brigands against the English soldiers, but the same powers of observation were not granted to English crimes against the common people.

The exact timeline of Wallace's evolution from solitary outlaw to militia leader is unknown, but the consensus is that his rise in prominence occurred between 1293 and 1296. During this time, he improved his swordsmanship and athletic prowess. More crucially, he turned into a powerful military strategist that could command a relatively large force of men and lead them toward a victory against the most successful army in all of Europe at the time. Despite his lack of wealth, noble standing, formal military experience, or land ownership, Wallace's impressive physique, unwavering willpower, and charisma were enough to propel his rise from fugitive to war hero.

Blind Harry details several of Wallace's exploits from his time as an outlaw. In one instance, Wallace decided to take up an English soldier/weightlifter's challenge to let anyone strike him across the back with a rough pole in Ayr. While in disguise, Wallace accepted his challenge and then broke his back with a single blow. He then quickly killed five other English soldiers while making his escape to Leglen Wood.

In another tale, the outcome veers far closer to tragedy. Wallace was in Aur once again and decided to intervene when one of Lord

Percy's men demanded a sheriff's servant to hand over a fish he had purchased for his master. Wallace killed him but was then overpowered by the sheer number of English soldiers who rushed to avenge their comrade. He was bound hand and foot and starved in a dungeon. By the time his trial came, he had contracted a fever and was in a deep coma. The English assumed he was dead and tossed his body over a wall, leaving him to rot in a heap of dung.

Thankfully, his first nurse at Ellerslie arrived and asked for the permission to give his body a proper burial. The soldiers agreed, leaving her to discover that he was still alive. She arranged for a fake wake to keep up the impression that he was dead, and secretly nursed him back to health. The news of Wallace's death became a matter of widespread significance when Thomas the Rhymer – a known prophet and soothsayer – prophesied that Wallace would play a pivotal role in restoring Scottish pride upon discovering that he was still alive:

"For sooth, ere he decease,

Shall many thousands in the field make end.

From Scotland he shall forth the Southron send,

And Scotland thrice he shall bring to peace.

So good of hand again shall ne'er be kenned[xxxiii]."

This was an age before science – an age of superstition and destiny. Thomas the Rhymer (Sir Thomas Rymour of Ercildoune) was in his seventies by this time and had accurately predicted the death of Alexander III, who had ill-fatedly decided to take a nighttime horse ride during a storm despite the prophecy of doom that hung over his head.[xxxiv] Having fought his way back to life from the dead, the prophecy would have surely empowered him with a sense of destiny and purpose. When Wallace made his recovery, he made his way to Glasgow by road with only a rusty blade for protection. Silver, horses, and armor were soon acquired by killing two English soldiers he met on the way.

He was reunited with his Uncle Richard at Riccarton. The lone outlaw was no more. As the prophesied savior of Scotland, he was joined by Sir Richard's three sons, Richard, Adam, and Simon, along with Robert Boyd of Kilmarnock and several other trusted companions. This band of brothers, nephews, uncles, cousins, and distant relatives formed a literal and figurative brotherhood that was wholly united against their formidable English foes. Wallace had become a Christ-like figure after narrowly escaping death; his fame inspired devotion, loyalty, and faith in the possibility of a victory. What the Scots lacked in technological sophistication and weaponry, they made up in zeal, inventiveness, and their acute knowledge of their home terrain.

Chapter 5 – Uprising

According to Blind Harry,[xxxv] Wallace seized the opportunity to avenge his father's death in 1297. Wallace learned that Fenwick, the knight who had killed his father, had returned to Scotland and was preoccupied with a mission in the southwest. He had been tasked with transporting large amounts of gold and silver (which had been confiscated from the Scottish churches) to Ayr. Wallace planned an ambush at Loudoun Hill.

When he emerged from the wood, he was no longer dressed in a disguise. He wore a secure armor, a small steel helmet, gloves made of plate cloth armor, a habergeon (a chainmail neck-covering that protected the breast), and a steel collar. Since his helmet was not closed, he had to protect his face with his armored hands.

Fenwick was accompanied by one hundred and eighty men, while Wallace was now the leader of fifty men.[xxxvi] He surprised the English horsemen by blocking the narrow pass with boulders and rocks. His men forced them to fight on foot by stabbing the horses in their unarmored belly. Wallace and his lieutenants quickly dispatched of the English leaders (including Fenwick), which then demoralized the surviving soldiers. Eighty of them successfully escaped, leaving a hundred of their comrades lying dead on the ground. Many had been trampled by the horses, which panicked after their rider was eliminated. Wallace lost three men and killed all his opponents. The English servants were marched to Clyde's Forest and hung, but he made sure that his men spared all women and children. His men then took possession of two hundred horses, the provisions and wine they carried, the Knights' armor, weapons, and money.

News of the victory spread across the countryside, where it was interpreted as a sign that the prophecy was being fulfilled. Fifty Scotsmen had successfully taken down nearly two hundred horsemen despite their heavy armor. The English soldiers no longer seemed as invincible as they had once been. Other patriotic-minded young men, fugitives, and men who resented English rule began to seek out the gigantic outlaw that served as a beacon of hope against English oppression.

Meanwhile, Lord Percy was being advised to establish a truce with the growing threat. It was not uncommon for Scottish magnates to switch allegiances after being promised generous wealth and large estates. Sir Ranald Craufurd was pressured to serve as an intermediary, since Wallace was his nephew. Wallace accepted the terms of the truce, which was to last for ten months. His men then went their separate ways.

He proved to be unsuited to a quiet and peaceful life. One day, he headed into town with fifteen of his allies in disguise. There, he spotted a passage-at-arms and a famed English champion who had defeated all of his opponents thus far. When Wallace secured a quick and effortless victory, the English soldiers realized that this unusually large man was the notorious outlaw. After a violent confrontation, Wallace and his allies escaped, leaving twenty-nine dead English soldiers in the market town. Lord Percy then insisted that Wallace stay out of the town, fair, or market to avoid confrontations with his soldiers.

When Sir Ranald was summoned to attend a council at Glasgow in September 1296, Wallace got into another confrontation with the English soldiers. While riding ahead of his uncle's entourage, he encountered a few of Percy's men. They demanded that Wallace hand over Sir Ranald's pack-horse to them, leaving him livid.

Wallace was further disgruntled when his uncle agreed to let the matter go. That night, he confronted the three horsemen and two-foot soldiers that had demanded the horse and killed them all with the help of two comrades. They returned with the horse, Percy's horses, harness, equipment, weapons, and money. The trio then headed to the safety of the mountains surrounding Loch Lomond.

At the council, Wallace was declared a formal outlaw and an enemy of King Edward. Sir Ranald and his troop were arrested and made to answer for the murder and robbery of Percy's men. The charges were dropped when he produced a solid alibi and insisted that he had no knowledge of Wallace's plans. He was forced to swear that he would not communicate with his nephew from that point onward.

Meanwhile, Wallace began recruiting more men until he had sixty of them under his command. With the help of his hardened fellow outlaws, he began to act as a Scottish Robin Hood. The English were killed and robbed. Their possessions were generously distributed to the Scots. Wallace headed toward the north, where he successfully captured the tower at Gargunnock. After four days, he and his men burned the castle and continued on their way to Strathearn. They killed every Englishman they met along the way.

His band of men took on Sir James Butler of Kinclaven and his men. Their numbers were evenly matched, but the English had the advantage of their horses and better armor. The Scots repeated their strategy at Loudoun Hill. By slashing at the horses' legs and bellies, they unseated the English riders and attacked them with their swords. Wallace himself slashed through Sir James' armor, cutting into his bone and brain. With their commander dead, many of the survivors panicked and fled. Wallace and his men followed them into the castle, where everyone – except the women, children, and two priests – was killed. After robbing the castle of its wealth, the survivors were freed and the castled was burned to the ground.

Lady Butler and the other survivors headed to Perth to raise the alarm. Wallace soon had a more formidable opponent: Sir Gerard

Heron and his thousand-man cavalry. Wallace braced himself for the assault, ready to make a stand. The Scots had precise aim, but the English archers had a seemingly endless supply of arrows. During the battle, Wallace himself suffered an arrow shot under the neck which left him with a permanent scar. With only fifty men left standing against the English forces (whose numbers had surged with the arriving reinforcements), Wallace urged his men to fight valiantly despite being outnumbered ten to one: "Here is no choice but either do or die. We have the right with us." In the end, they were forced to retreat into the deepest and thickest parts of the woods. After a few more scuffles, they managed to escape.

After a few more close calls with the English forces, Wallace was left with only a tiny cohort. The stories about their efforts nevertheless traveled across the country, inspiring the same dedication to resistance in the minds and hearts of their countrymen. Aggrieved by the deaths of many of his comrades, Wallace kept a low profile. Blind Harry nevertheless reports that he still killed any Englishmen he encountered (in areas where there were fewer English patrolmen) during this interim period.

Chapter 6 – Love in a Time of War

In Mel Gibson's 1995 Hollywood blockbuster film *Braveheart*,[xxxvii] Wallace's transformation into a legendary hero is catalyzed by the death of his wife. Her name in the movie is Murron MacClannough, and she is portrayed by English actress Catherine McCormack. The idea of Wallace being inspired to lead his countrymen to achieve a decisive victory against the English by the attempted rape and murder of his wife is certainly highly symbolic. Her body thus becomes a vivid and visceral metaphor for the nation of Scotland itself.

The historical reality is probably far less poetic and simple. Wallace had certainly already been dedicated to opposing the English forces long before he fell in love. The original Blind Harry poem makes no mention of a wife, although it does refer to a woman named Innes. Innes is credited for helping him escape from the English troops; Blind Harry does not mention that she was his wife or lover.

In a 1570 revised edition of Blind Harry's poem, the eighteen-year-old Marion Braidfute makes her first appearance as William Wallace's wife. The plot is simple and symbolic: the Sheriff of Lanark murders Marion, encouraging Wallace to lead a successful rebellion against the English. Some historians have argued that Marion is a fictional character who was invented to support a noble family's claim to be Wallace's descendants. The revised edition conveniently mentions that Marion gave birth to a daughter before being murdered by the sheriff. Her name – which seems to draw a parallel to Robin Hood's love interest Maid Marian (or Marion) – also seems to be too symbolically convenient.

Myth or fact, Marion endures because her existence makes Wallace's narrative more compelling. According to Blind Harry, Marion herself bore a deep resentment against the English for her older brother's death. Wallace supposedly fell in love at first sight when he saw her at the Church of Saint Kentigern, near Lanark. Despite deeming marriage in the time of war to be imprudent, Wallace began seeing Marion in secret whenever he came to town. To make matters even more imprudent, Sir William Heselrig, the English sheriff of Lanark, was interested in having Marion marry his son.

Blind Harry reports that Wallace planned to marry Marion once he had freed Scotland from English rule. In another part of the poem, however, he contradicts this pact and reveals that they did get married and produced a daughter who then married a squire named Shaw, thus preserving Wallace's lineage. Several historians – including Dr Charles Rogers – have dismissed all claims that Wallace married or had any children, illegitimate or otherwise.[xxxviii]

In any case, Blind Harry reports that Sir William Heselrig, Sheriff of Clydesdale, accosted Wallace one Sunday morning as he left Saint Kentigern's Church. After a series of insults, Wallace and his men began fighting with Heselrig's men. Wallace had purportedly married Marion by this time, and he took refuge in her house after the Scots were forced to retreat. Heselrig and his men eventually marched up to Marion's door, demanding Wallace's surrender. Marion killed time by arguing with him, allowing Wallace to escape out the back door. When they realized what was going on, they smashed through the door and killed her then and there.

Wallace's own mother is believed to have died around this time period, creating a strong emotional incentive for him to strike a deadly blow at the English. Whatever his actual motivations and intentions, Wallace did successfully murder Sir William Heselrig in May 1297. That very night, Wallace and his men returned to town. Wallace made a straight line for the sheriff's home and found his target in the bedroom. With a single downward stroke, he cut through Heselrig's skull, right down to the collarbone. The fact that he cut the sheriff to pieces does suggest that there was a personal vendetta that had to be settled, but perhaps he was only making an example out of him to strike fear in the English forces. After killing Heselrig's son, he burned the house and its remaining inhabitants. Wallace and his men then took the opportunity to kill many Englishmen that night – approximately 240 were murdered.

Unlike Blind Harry's reports of Wallace's exploits, the carnage at Lanark is supported by Wallace's trial documents. Wallace was specifically charged with murdering the Sheriff of Clydesdale, presumably as a symbolic action that instigated the various resistance efforts that coalesced into the first Scottish War of Independence. There had been many uprisings and revolts before this, of course, but none of them matched the scale and severity of Heselrig's murder and the Lanark massacre.

Chapter 7 – The Battle of Stirling Bridge

Wallace quickly fled to the familiar territory of Ayrshire after the Lanark massacre. Scottish men from the southwest rallied to his side, reuniting Wallace with old comrades and many fresh faces. The revolutionary spirit had been kindled, and Wallace now had the benefit of all the weapons and armor he had taken from the defeated English soldiers. At this point, he was in charge of three thousand men with decent weaponry, as well as many men without the benefit of horses and military equipment.

Gilbert de Grimsby (who was known to the Scots as Jop) had also joined Wallace's ranks. As a well-regarded soldier who had served in the English army and been recognized by no less than King Edward himself, his defection was a severe blow to the English forces. Besides his own skills and military prowess, he arrived with critical intelligence about the English army and its inner workings. Wallace happily made him his standard-bearer.

The flames of revolt were also stirred by the Robert Wishart (the Bishop of Glasgow) and James the Steward. Both men had been elected Guardians of Scotland in 1286. Wishart was opposed to Edward's attempts to anglicize the Scottish Church. This involved the replacement of Scottish clergy members with English priests. Unlike the Scottish magnates, the clergymen had no land and wealth interests to protect. Wallace certainly benefited from Wishart's network of like-minded clergymen who could use the cover of the church for covert anti-English activities and communication. With Wishart's backing, Wallace's revolt was "justified" as a legitimate war in the name of King John.

Wallace did not have to wait long for action. After he was released from confinement in late 1296, Sir Willian Douglas (previously governor of Berwick Castle) swiftly allied himself with the rebels. He attacked and captured the Sanquhar castle, and then had to defend it against the Captain of Durisdeer. Wallace rushed to the scene to aid him, killing five hundred English soldiers as a result. Edward responded by stripping Douglas of his property and lands in Northumberland and Essex. This did not stop other prominent Scottish figures – like Robert Bruce, the future King of Scotland – from defecting to the rebels.

Wallace also discovered that he had a counterpart in the northern part of the country. Andrew de Moray had decided to stage a rash revolt after his father and uncle (Sir Andrew de Moray and Sir William) were taken prisoner after the Battle of Dunbar. By April 1297, the entire area of Moray was united in opposing the English. Given that the Moray family had the same name as the region they lived in, it is no surprise that they were a powerful family with massive estates and influence. Moray and his men began attacking the English garrisons in the northeast and were eventually emboldened to attack Urquhart Castle.

Edward was away while all this was happening, and the Englishman that was nominally in charge of Scotland while he was away was Hugh Cressingham (who was based in Berwick). Luckily for the Scots, Cressingham did not carry out Edward's orders properly. There were still no stone walls at Berwick; some suspected that Cressingham was pocketing the funds for the project.

That June, Wallace raided Perth with the help of Sir Willian Douglas. Despite being at the center of the English regime in

Scotland, the English defenders of Perth were forced to retreat as the Scottish army advanced. Large amounts of chattels and goods were left behind for Wallace to claim. By the end of the month, English troops in the southern part of the country had all retreated into their castles. The Scottish armed rebels roamed the countryside, confining the English to the towns and burghs. They were constantly under siege from the Scot rebels; the tables had been turned. Four critical figures were deemed to be responsible for Scotland's increasingly anarchic state: the Bishop of Glasgow, James the Steward, Andrew de Moray, and William Wallace.

Edward retaliated by ordering that all rebels be arrested and imprisoned. He rallied an army of three thousand horsemen and forty thousand footmen in the north of England and sent them across the Scottish border. Instead of fighting, the Scottish army surrendered on 7 July. The Scottish magnates were unable to establish an effective chain of command and agree on the army's leadership structure.

The magnates may have spontaneously collapsed, but Wallace's rebel army was there to stay. They attacked Lord Percy's forces with guerilla tactics, killing over five hundred English soldiers.[xxxix] The Scottish nobles had failed to defend their country's honor, leaving Wallace and Moray to capture to lead the revolution. Wallace confronted Lord Percy's forces at Glasgow and managed to secure a victory by the middle of the day. By the end of the month, Cressingham was writing to Edward for additional funds to cope with the widespread defiance in the country. Raising the money by taxing the Scottish people was certainly not an option by now:

> Sire, let it not displease you, by far the greater part of your counties of the realm of Scotland are still unprovided with keepers, as well by death, siege, or imprisonment; and some have given up their bailiwicks, and others neither will nor dare return; and in some counties the Scots have established and placed bailiffs and ministers, so that no county is in proper order, except Berwick and Roxburgh, and this only lately.[xl]

When August 1297 drew to a close, the northern part of Scotland had largely been reclaimed by Wallace and his army of rebels. Perth and Aberdeen had been easily conquered. The only exceptions were the well-defended strongholds of Dundee and Stirling. Edward ordered John de Warenne – the Earl of Surrey and Governor in Scotland for Edward – to provide additional reinforcements at Stirling and to raise the siege of Dundee.[xli] As Wallace attempted to subdue the English forces at Dundee, he learned that Warenne and Cressingham were leading a large army northward toward Stirling.[xlii]

Stirling is located in a central position in Scotland, making it strategically crucial. Stirling Castle was then one of the most formidable castles in the entire British Isles, perched on top of a large crag that oversaw the vast surrounding plains. The River Forth meandered through this plain, making its way toward the Scots Sea. Stirling was the gateway to the Highlands, and the English intended to recapture it to reestablish their control over the north. Led by Warenne, the English cavalry and infantry advanced toward Stirling Castle. Confident of the English army's superior numbers, weaponry, and logistics, he predicted that Wallace and Andrew de Moray's rebellion would end by defeat in battle or negotiation. His Scottish opponents were based on the Abbey Craig, which is home to the National Wallace Monument today.

The English forces eventually arrived at a narrow, wooden bridge that crossed the River Forth. The Stirling Bridge that exists today is in a different location from this original bridge. The old bridge was supported by 8 piers and was actually diagonal. The bridge was only wide enough to allow two horsemen to pass through abreast. Warenne's entire cavalry (1,000 men) and infantry (15,000 men) would have taken a few hours to get to the other side. They would then be forced to enter a narrow bend in the river, leaving them vulnerable to attacks from the side.

Given the disadvantageous terrain, Warrene did not order his troops to cross the bridge immediately. For a few days, both forces remained on opposite banks of the river. Warrene expected Wallace and Moray to surrender without a fight. He was surprised when they refused to admit defeat despite the recent English victories and their obvious military advantages. The two Dominican friars he sent across to bridge to negotiate surrender from Wallace returned with a call for confrontation: "Tell your commander that we are not here to make peace but to do battle, defend ourselves and liberate our kingdom. Let them come on, and we shall prove this in their very beards."[xliii]

This was certainly a brave decision. An army made up of common men had never stood up against the might of the English army before this. The forces that were led by Scottish nobility had all been defeated thus far. Wallace and Mornay were both young and experienced. The odds were against them, but they were willing to risk everything. All of them possessed a determination to bring English tyranny in their country to an end. They had endured the English soldier's brutality, arrogance, rudeness, and imperiousness over the past seven years; it was time to attempt to bring that era to an abrupt end.

Finally convinced that Wallace and Mornay would not surrender, Warenne ordered his troops to cross the bridge on the morning of the 11th of September. Warenne had considered sending his horsemen upstream to the Ford of Drip, so that they could provide protection to his footmen as they crossed the bridge. This idea was suggested by Sir Richard Lundie, a Scottish noble who had switched allegiances at the battle of Irvine:

> My lords, if we go on to the bridge we are dead men; for we cannot cross it except two by two, and the enemy are on our flank, and can come down on us as they will, all in one front. But there is a ford not far from here, where we can cross sixty at a time. Let me now therefore have five hundred knights and a small body of infantry, and we will get round the enemy on the rear and crush them; and meanwhile you, my Lord Earl, and the others who are with you, will cross the bridge in perfect safety.[xliv]

This plan was foiled by Cressingham, who lamented the fact that a large amount of money had already been spent to subdue the revolution. The English army was to cross immediately and acquire a swift victory. When more than half of the English army had crossed over to the other side, Wallace and Moray set the trap they had planned into action. Armed with long spears, the Scottish rebels charged down the causeway at the sound of Wallace's horn. The right flank of the charge made their way across the river bank to arrive at the bridge's north end, thus preventing the English army from retreating to safety. The English army was now trapped, but one group of English knights managed to fight their way back across the bridge. The archers would have been able to assist the English forces by firing from the other side of the river, but they had unfortunately already crossed the bridge by this point. Warenne had wisely waited to cross the bridge, and had it destroyed before retreating to Berwick.

The rest of the English army who had crossed over was then forced to defend themselves against the Scottish onslaught. Some were able to swim to safety, while others were weighted down by the heavy armor and drowned, and the large majority were killed in the massacre. Hugh de Cressingham, who had crossed first, was killed alongside the rest. From their higher vantage point on the slope, the Scottish rebels aimed their spears and other missiles onto the advancing English knights. The knights that survived were soon disoriented when they reached the marshy ground on the other side, a location which severely compromised their horses.

It was a momentous victory. Five thousand English soldiers have been killed, while the rest retreated. The well-armed and mounted English knight had been proven to be fallible at the battlefield after all and at the hands of a ragtag group of spearmen that consisted mostly of commoners. Scotland had not achieved victory against a significant English army since the times of the Dark Ages. The Battle of Stirling Bridge thus proved to be a potent catalyst for the ongoing resistance against Edward's imposition. Wallace's victory was not without casualties, however. Andrew Mornay was fatally wounded during the battle. He survived for two months before being buried at the Fortrose Cathedral.[xlv]

Chapter 8 – Invading England

The Battle of Stirling Bridge may have been a momentous event, but it was not enough to single-handedly force Edward to retire his designs on Scotland. Wallace's unexpected victory also created further divisions between his guerilla forces and the Scottish nobility. It was no secret that the Scottish magnates had been motivated more by their own interests rather than an inspiring sense of patriotism, and Wallace's newfound influence threatened to further weaken their positions in the eyes of the Scottish commoners.

There was nevertheless a brief window when Wallace commanded the support of Scots across all class lines. He wasted no time in attacking the remaining pockets of English resistance after his victory of Stirling. The English forces at Dundee had already learned of their counterparts' crushing defeat at Stirling and surrendered soon after Wallace and his men arrived. He then set his sights on reclaiming the rest of Scotland's rigorously fortified castles: Cupar Castle, Edinburg Castle, Dunbar Castle, Berwick Castle, and Roxburgh Castle. Wallace's forces were unable to force the defenders of the latter four castles to surrender, but they were able to force the English army out of their respective towns.

By October, Wallace had been successful in driving a large majority of the English army out of Scotland. A few castles and strongholds remained under English control, but they now exerted negligible power over the Scottish populace. This astounding achievement –

which Wallace pulled off without much help from the Scottish nobility – established his reputation as a powerful general and a rising political force. In truth, Wallace's victory was shared with Andrew de Moray. Both young men were the sons of knights, but the latter was in possession of substantial lands, a status indicator that mattered significantly during the thirteenth century. With Andrew on his deathbed, however, Wallace was the sole claimant of the spoils.

As the de facto leader of Scotland, Wallace quickly communicated with Scotland's trading partners to let them know that "the kingdom of Scotland is recovered by war from the power of the English" and was ready to resume business. Wallace might have won over the common people at this point, but he still faced the difficult task of establishing an alliance with the great Scottish magnates. Some were converts to his cause, others were ambivalent, and a few were determined to support Edward. Wallace mobilized his forces to attack Earl Patrick, a staunch Edward supporter who had refused to swear his loyalty to Scotland and insulted Wallace when summoned to do so.

Once Earl Patrick had been defeated, Wallace and his forces were free to turn the tables on Berwick, which had become an English settlement after its harrowing defeat the previous year. Wallace repaid the bloody favor by allowing his army to turn the town into a scene of carnage once again. After Berwick, the Scottish forces advanced into Northumberland and Cumbria. Many Northumbrians had fled to Newcastle, which offered the protection of its fortified walls, after witnessing the once-proud and indestructible English army fleeing southward in an alarmingly disorganized manner. Since they had taken their cattle and their valuables with them, the Scots were greeted with empty farmhouses and cottages. These were quickly burned to the ground by the angry Scots.

At Cumbria, Wallace's men had to be more strategic. Instead of indiscriminate destruction, they claimed all the food they could find. Meanwhile, the Northumbrians returned to their villages and farms, as they believed that the Scottish forces had moved on. When

Wallace learned of their return, he ordered his men to greet the English villagers with a nasty surprise. All the Englishmen that lived in Northumbria paid dearly for the atrocities their countrymen had inflicted on Berwick, even though they had nothing to do with the massacre.

Wallace had no intentions of ordering his men to attack the castles that were occupied by the English forces, but Carlisle was an exception. Its strategic position as the western entry point to Scotland made it crucial in tipping the balance of military power between Wallace's army and the English army. He sent a large force to surround it, but they made no major attempt to attack its inhabitants. The rest of Wallace's vagrant army headed to Newcastle. There, they burned the small town of Ritton to the ground after its villagers made the painful mistake of taunting the Scots from across the river, not assuming that the Scots would simply swim across it.

By now, Wallace's attempt to avenge his fallen countrymen by attacking the north of England had thoroughly demoralized the northern English people. Over seven hundred English villages were burned down without mercy or remorse; Wallace's forces killed thousands of defenseless people. Those that remained had no courage or conviction to resist or defy the Scottish invaders. The Scottish army thus had free reign to strip the villages of towns of most of their food and valuable possessions.

The Scots' presence in northern England was nevertheless short-lived. Not long before Christmas that year, the English led a counterattack against the Scots. Under Sir Robert de Clifford's instructions, several thousand English foot soldiers killed over three hundred Scotsmen at Annandale. By the time they took a break for Christmas, ten villages and towns had been razed. They resumed their attacks the next year, claiming the town of Annan and destroying the Gisburn church. Civilians on both sides of the Scottish border suffered disproportionately during this time.

Chapter 9 – The Guardian of Scotland

The historical record on who actually knighted Wallace is unclear, but he was knighted Guardian of Scotland sometime around the Christmas period of 1297. Wallace was probably knighted by a member of the Scottish nobility or a powerful magnate; this may have been James the Steward or Malcolm, Earl of Lennox. In any case, Wallace now had the power to act on behalf of the entire Scottish realm and with the consent and support of the magnates. Some of the magnates undoubtedly bore some opposition to the idea of a young man of dubious standing becoming the sole ruler of Scotland, but he had won the confidence of the people and had a victorious army behind him.

At the dawn of 1298, Wallace was at the peak of his military and political career. He had an unexpected victory against the most powerful army in Europe under his belt and had returned from his northern invasion of England with large bounties of cattle, grain, and other precious food commodities. A giant in body, spirit, and reputation, he had an enviable image as a selfless patriot who had dedicated his entire life to a vision of an independent and proud Scotland. Meanwhile, the Scottish nobility – the knights, earls, and barons – had been severely discredited by their notoriously shaky allegiances.

Wallace was thus at the helm of a disorganized and divided nation, wrought by feudal hierarchies and endless infighting. As a political leader, he demonstrated the same capacity for decisive and immediate action that he showcased on the battlefield. The magnates that did not gratefully heed his commands were ruthlessly cowed into submission. At the end of the day, however, none of the Scottish earls were willing to pledge their undivided support. Blinded by envy and wounded by the idea of being outranked by a commoner, they could not put aside their self-interests to support the interests of the public.

Their temporary allegiance to Wallace was nevertheless unwavering enough to prevent them from attending a parliament session called by Edward on 14 January 1298. Their absence – which effectively marked them as public enemies of England – indicated the extent to which Edward's grip over Scotland had waned. The loyalties of England's own magnates to Edward were also under major strain. The English earls did attend that parliament session, but they were indignant at the cost that Edward's foreign invasions had inflicted upon them. Edward himself was absent, leaving behind a power vacuum that nearly led to a revolt.

Edward began raising money to pay for an imposing attack against Wallace. Welsh troops were mobilized for a decisive retaliation. By 22 January, the English magnates estimated that they had an army of fourteen thousand horsemen and a hundred thousand foot soldiers assembled, the largest army to be amassed against the Scots thus far. Anxious to redeem himself after the disastrous Battle of Stirling Bridge, Earl Warenne led the second charge into Scotland. The sheer size of the English army secured a quick victory at Roxburgh. Warenne then advanced to Kelso, where the presence of Wallace's cavalry halted their progress into the hills. They then headed to Berwick, where they were graced with another quick surrender. At Berwick, Edward communicated to Warenne that he was returning to England to take supreme command over the Scottish invasion. Warenne was to stay put until he returned.

The winter of 1297-98 was a decisive period for both sides. Wallace organized Scotland into military districts and began conscripting all able-bodied Scottish males that were older than sixteen. He established a proper chain of command that borrowed from classical Rome and Greece, doing away with the former feudal arrangements that accorded greater military prestige to the landowning classes. Instead of appointing lower-ranked members of the nobility to the clergy, military, administrators, and law enforcement, Wallace began to recruit common men like himself on the basis of their merit. He erected gallows in every town, village, and burgh – a warning of what would befall those who failed to heed his conscription regulations.

The clergy was not spared from Wallace's zeal for reform. He appointed William de Lamberton to become the head of St. Andrews, rewarding him for his early support. With his nominee in a place of power, Wallace eliminated all the English priests that Edward had installed. These English priests and nuns were forcibly removed from their positions, and some of them were killed in the process.

Most of Wallace's efforts were ultimately focused on the upcoming confrontation with Edward. Wallace had devised and perfected a new military formation to battle the English by this point: the schiltrom. His foot soldiers would utilize their impressive twelve-foot spears to form an intimidating hedgehog-like formation, with spears posed in all directions. Protected by their shields, the Scottish infantry would be better placed to confront the feared English cavalry at close quarters.

As the English army drew closer, Wallace ordered that the towns in the Lothians and Berwickshire be destroyed. All the Scottish people in these areas were evacuated to the north, leaving behind a barren countryside. King Edward returned to England as promised and began laying down meticulous plans after testing the strength of the Scottish defenses and the will of the people to resist his massive army. There were several smaller raids and conflicts before the main invasion on 25 June. To prepare for a final and utter victory over Wallace's forces, Edward arranged for provisions to be transported from Ireland to a depot at Carlisle. Supplies were amassed at ports in eastern England, ready to be shipped into Berwick and Edinburgh once they had been reclaimed.

When Edward arrived at Roxburgh on 24 June, the English army was composed of three thousand heavy cavalrymen, four thousand light horsemen, and eighty thousand foot soldiers. A majority of the footmen were hired troops from Ireland and Wales, rather than conscripted Englishmen. Edward rode ahead of this sizable army, witnessing firsthand the preemptive devastation that awaited the English at the burned ruins of the villages and farms throughout the Lothians. After putting up a fight, the castle of Dirletons (located near the coast of East Lothian) and Tantallon were conquered. The English army then marched into the heart of Scotland, ready to attack in any direction upon knowledge of where Wallace's army was located.

Chapter 10 – Defeat at Falkirk

A large army comes with massive logistical problems. As the head of approximately 87,500 men, Edward had the difficult task of ensuring that there were sufficient food supply channels to feed all of them. As they marched further into Scotland, it was severely demoralizing to witness the extent of Wallace's scorched earth strategy. The only food source that the English troops had access to came from the supply ships, which were often compromised by itinerant weather and Scottish pirates. When Edward attempted to placate the troops by distributing two hundred casks of wine (a few supply ships had arrived with ample alcohol and little food), this lead to drunken infighting between the Welsh and Englishmen. Hunger had led the morale of the English army to reach a dangerously low point.

For now, Wallace's strategy of buying his time was working. The English army was fatigued after making many long marches throughout the Scottish countryside, without being able to engage the Scottish army in any meaningful confrontation. Edward eventually ordered his men to withdraw to Edinburgh and wait for their food supplies to be restocked. On 21 July, a scout reported that Wallace's army had been sighted nearby – eighteen miles away in the Forest of Selkirk. Wallace was evidently waiting for the English to retreat before launching his offensive.

Edward made plans for an immediate confrontation. By 9 a.m. that day, the English troops were marching toward Falkirk.[xlvi] They arrived at Linlithgow by nightfall. The next day, they spotted the presence of a Scottish cavalry patrol. The morning sun had reflected off their spears, emitting a telltale flash. The Scots were nowhere to be found by the time the English arrived at the location, but Edward knew that the Scottish army was close by.

In retrospect, it was ill-advised for Wallace to abandon his guerrilla tactics in favor of a direct confrontation at this point. This may not have been Wallace's intention; it could very well be that the English surprised him with their willingness to march through the night. Falkirk was surrounded by more open country, making a retreat much more treacherous than in hillside terrain. Whatever the reason, Wallace ordered his troops to assemble in battle formation in a strategic location.

Historians have hazarded that the battle took place north of the actual town, on particularly marshy terrain that thwarted the English horsemen. Wallace expected a familiar set-up: his spear-armed infantry against the English's heavily armed horsemen. At Stirling, his men had been on the offensive. Here, they would be on the defensive. The site of the battle was not as advantageous as that fateful narrow bridge, but the marshes and woods did offer protection if retreat was necessary.

What Wallace could not have expected, however, was the deadliness of the Welshmen and Lancastrians' longbow. This was a recent invention that was as revolutionary to medieval warfare as poison gas had been to early twentieth century warfare. Without the deadly range and aim of the English archers, Edward's troops would likely have been thwarted by the forest of spears that the Scotsmen had organized.

As the English army drew near, Wallace compelled his men to courageous action: "I have brought you to the ring; dance the best you can!"[xlvii] Edward initially ordered that the Welshmen be sent first into battle with the Scots, but they refused to be used as guinea pigs. In the end, the English cavalry was sent to do battle with Wallace's men, only to be surprised by the swampy grounds which had been camouflaged by the green meadow. They were forced to free themselves from the bog and find their way around it.

The second line of cavalry advanced more warily. They headed in a diagonal direction toward the eastern side of the swamp. Once they crossed the stream, they waited for the third line – led by Edward himself – to advance. Wallace's schiltroms were prepared for all four lines of English cavalry. His footmen were disciplined enough to hold tight to their spears and armor as the armed English knights advanced, forcing them to wheel about without striking the Scots.

Unable to confront the Scottish infantry, the English cavalry turned their attention toward the Scottish archers. While over a hundred English horses were claimed by the Scots spears, the English knights made quick work of the Scottish archers. Edward then ordered the core of his infantry to attack. Their ranks contained a sizable number of Lancastrian longbowmen who were able to attack where the cavalry could not reach. They summoned forth a fatal hail of arrows, backed by the flurry of stones and rocks hurled forward by the foot soldiers. The seemingly impregnable schiltroms began to flounder as they were showered with arrows and projectiles. As they abandoned their ranks and fled, the English cavalry moved in with a deadly charge. The twelve-foot spears were practically useless in close combat.

Covered by the dense woods, Wallace and the surviving members of his army retreated to the north. Upon witnessing the infantry's crushing defeat, the Scottish cavalry had wisely decided to flee to live and fight the English another day. The retreating Scottish foot soldiers were given no quarters by the English knights. Those who escaped the deadly lances were also at risk at drowning when they attempted to cross the River Carron. By the end of the chase, nearly ten thousand Scottish foot soldiers have been killed. Nearly every family in southern Scotland would have suffered grief due to this catastrophic defeat. Wallace was left without an infantry, and without his reputation as an effective Scottish leader that stood a chance of freeing Scotland from English influence. His government – which lasted for three hundred days – was brought to an abrupt end. He lived on long after Falkirk was over (unlike in the Hollywood movie, which had him tried and executed soon after this defeat), but his ability to influence Scottish affairs had been maimed.

Chapter 11 – An Outlaw Once More

Wallace gave up his guardianship soon after the Battle of Falkirk. It is not known whether this was voluntary or otherwise. In any case, his position of leadership had been severely compromised by the crushing defeat at Falkirk, despite the fact that he could not have possibly foreseen the novel deadliness of the English longbow at the time. He marched north to Stirling, where he arranged for the town and castle to be destroyed – rather than let it fall into English hands. He repeated this strategy in Perth, forcing the English to rely solely on the food brought in by their supply ships.

In August, Edward advanced into an empty and burned Ayr, without having managed to lay his hands on Wallace. When the supply ships he expected from Ireland and west England failed to arrive, his army suffered from a fifteen-day famine. By the next month, Edward had abandoned all his plans to wipe out the Scottish resistance forces. Instead, he began garrisoning various strongpoints to help cement his reign of power in Scotland.

Edward returned to England on 8 September, disappointed by the costs he had endured to achieve the victory at Falkirk. He had lost a large number of men to illness, starvation, and disease. Only a small number of his horses had returned safely to Carlisle. His troops had been on the verge of mutiny due to the lack of food, and he had not managed to destroy the Scottish rebels after all. There were, however, some consolations. They divided the estates of the Scottish barons who had failed to demonstrate their loyalties, and then restored the English clergy who had been removed from their positions in Scotland.

The worse blow was the discovery that some of Scottish magnates (e.g. Sir Simon Fraser) that had previously been very loyal to Edward were now changing sides. The English may have defeated Wallace's men, but they had also been forced into a humiliating retreat. The Scottish spirit of resistance was still burning strongly, its heat rising from the common people to the ranks of the Scottish nobility. Edward certainly did not resign himself to this state of affairs. He began making plans for another intervention, "to go forward in the Scottish business upon the enemies of the crown and realm of England, and to put down their disobedience and their malice which purpose nothing else but to subdue the said crown, and the estate of the said realm of England, to their power."[xlviii]

Meanwhile, Wallace had melted into the woods once again, with his brother, Sir Malcolm, the Earl of Atholl, and a few other knights. Now that he could no longer lead the Scottish rebels in open warfare against Edward's forces, he had to revert back to the guerrilla tactics that he had mastered during his earlier years. His influence and impact were severely limited after the Battle of Falkirk, but he persevered instead of surrendering or admitting defeat. The duties of the Guardian of Scotland were shared by four figures during this time: Sir Robert de Keith, Sir David de Graham, and Sir William de Balliol, as well as the enigmatic James the Steward. With the Scottish magnates in the highest positions of power, the other earls, barons, and knights had less reason to oppose or undermine them. Wallace may have been removed from the picture, but he had triggered a rejuvenated sense of patriotism in the nation's traditional ruling classes.

Despite the ambivalent feelings that the Scottish elite held toward Wallace, there was no denying that he had proven to the entire nation that the Scottish spirit stood a chance against the most powerful army in all of Europe. Courage, determination, and strategic usage of the land were evidently potent enough to thwart and usurp Edward's obnoxious and intolerable subjugation of the country. If a relatively unknown man with no land to his name was brave enough to stand up against the English, why should the Scottish nobility be unable to match – or surpass – him? All they needed to do was to be united in arms against a common foe.

It is not known if Wallace had much or any faith in the ability of the new Guardians to resist and defy Edward. Whatever his outlook, it was evident that the highlight of his life and career had occurred in 1299; everything that followed appeared to be anticlimactic. Historian Ronald McNair-Scott dismissively characterized the last seven years of Wallace's life as obscure and impotent. Wallace was reduced to "harrying the English whenever he could with bands of fearless men or acting as messenger to the King of France or His Holiness the Pope for his friend William Lamberton, Bishop of St Andrews."xlix The full scope of Wallace's actions is not known, but there is sufficient documentation to demonstrate that Wallace benefited from having previously secured William de Lamberton's election to the bishopric of St. Andrews. Lamberton maintained his friendship with Wallace after the latter resigned from his Guardianship and proceeded to entrust him with diplomatic missions of the highest order.

As a diplomat, Wallace's ultimate goal was to secure the alliance of a powerful foreign nation that could help Scotland fend off Edward's plans to dominate it. Lamberton, Wallace, and a few other companions successfully evaded the English ships to sail to France and back. They were warmly received by King Philip, although the monarch did not explicitly promise to support Scotland with the French army or by allocating any significant financial resources to Scotland's fight for independence. Instead, Philip left them with a letter that praised "their constancy to their king and their shining valor in defense of their native land against injustice," and claimed that he was "not unmindful of the old league between their king, themselves, and him, and carefully pondering ways and means of helping them."[l]

Wallace was also singled out by the French monarch in a personal letter for his undying efforts to resist Edward's intimidating forces:

> Philip, by the grace of God, King of the French, to my loved and faithful, my agents, appointed to the Roman court, greetings and love: We command you to request the supreme Pontiff to hold our loved William the Waleis, of Scotland, knight, recommended to his favor, in those things which with him he has to dispatch. Given at Pierrefonds, on Monday after the feast of All Saints.[li]

After leaving France, Wallace headed to Norway and Rome with the intention of securing the alliance of Eric II and the Pope. Wallace's diplomatic efforts did not go unnoticed by Edward. Bishop Lamberton had made a direct appeal to the papacy, and Scotland's quest for sovereign status had been treated with sympathy. By 1302, Edward was anxious at the prospect of a Scottish victory and the return of the exiled John Balliol as the King of Scotland.

This did not come to be. The Scottish elites' inability to put forth a united front proved to be highly detrimental to the entire nation once again. The Comyns, who were supporters of Balliol, effectively sidelined the Bruces. When faced with the unwanted likelihood of Balliol returning to rule Scotland, they defected to Edward I. Scotland's diplomatic efforts also proved to be at an end. The Pope needed Edward's assistance in his latest crusade against Islam to a greater degree than he needed the Scots. After his first wife, Eleanor, died in 1290, Edward negotiated a peace treaty with France and sealed it with his marriage to Marguerite, King Philip's seventeen-year-old sister. When King Philip and Pope Boniface[lii] engaged in an open war against each other, Lamberton could have only reacted in dismay (the Pope was eventually captured by the French and put to death). Balliol had to consign himself with the realization that his return was illusory after all by 1304. Fatigued by a crushing diplomatic defeat and seven years of war (Edward had been sending his troops to attack Scotland every year), the Scottish nobility were ready to cut a deal with Edward.

Edward was in an indulgent and relatively generous state of mind as he accepted the Scottish's leaders' submission to him. He rewarded the Scottish magnates that submitted to his rule with public offices in Scotland, eager to obtain their loyalty in reward. He had hoped that Wallace himself would swear allegiance, but Wallace and his followers were willing to stand alone in their defiance. Angered by the capitulation he witnessed all around him, Wallace bravely maintained his stance as a patriot of the highest order:

> Scotland, desolate as you are, you believe too much in false words and are too unwary of woes to come! If you think like me, you would not readily place your neck under a foreign yoke. When I was growing up I learned from a priest who was my uncle to set this one proverb above all worldly possessions, and I have carried it in my heart,
>
> *I tell you the truth, freedom is the finest of things;*
>
> *Never live under a servile yoke, my son.*
>
> And that is why I tell you briefly that even if all Scots obey the King of England so that each one abandons his liberty, I and my companions who wish to be associated with me in this matter shall stand up for the liberty of the kingdom. And (may God be favorable to us!) we others shall obey no one but the King [of Scots] or his lieutenant.[liii]

Chapter 12 – The Execution

Edward placed a bounty of three hundred marks on Wallace's head. When Bishop Lamberton (Wallace's old friend and loyal ally) and Sir Simon Fraser also submitted to Edward, Wallace had no powerful allies left. With a reward on his head and antagonism from all the Scottish nobles who had capitulated to English rule, Wallace had abysmal chances at defeating the English army in battle.

Wallace and his band of guerrillas were violently defeated in a battle with a large English force led by Sir William de Latimer at Happrew, Sir John de Segrave, and Sir Robert de Clifford (near Stobo). The defeat was made all the more bitter by the fact that it was a Scotsman who had tracked Wallace down for the promise of a financial reward from Edward. This was Wallace's final battle. He was in no position to help Stirling Castle – the last Scottish stronghold holding out against the English – defend itself from a full-forced English assault.

On the 1st of April 1304, Edward ordered that Stirling Castle be blockaded, preventing its defenders from gaining access to crucial provisions. Formidable siege-engines were shipped from Edinburgh to Berwick; the castle's formidable defenses would soon have to contend with the greatest artillery in the entire English Isles. On 22 April, Edward himself arrived at Stirling to lead the siege operations. He had thirteen of the most powerful devices engineered at the time, each capable of hurling forth a stone or rock that was up to three hundred pounds over a distance of a thousand yards. There was also a crane with a mobile platform that could hoist a cage of twenty men over the castle walls. Other specialized machines were equipped to pull down parapets and galleries, while others were designed to ram through gates and walls.

The defenders of Stirling Castle had no intentions of going down without a fight. They lowered grapnels from the walls with cranes, overturning Edward's specialized machines. Molten lead and boiling oil rained down on the English army. Edward himself was shot by a Scottish archer but was saved by his armor. The English army was also plagued by the same lack of food as the Scottish defenders; their horses had to subsist on grass alone. On 20 July 1304, the Scottish rebels finally succumbed to Edward's demand for an absolute and unconditional surrender. Sir William Oliphant was imprisoned in the Tower of London, leaving Wallace standing alone as the country's last great patriot. Edward offered fairly lenient terms to the Scottish magnates that had opposed him. They were humiliated in public, banished for a few years, or sent into exile.

While Edward tightened his grip over the country with a more intrusive military and administrative occupation, Wallace led his band of outlaws through the countryside. Their main concerns were survival. They had to secure enough supplies while eluding the English army and Scotsmen eager to turn them in for Edward's bounty. Edward may have been merciful to the magnates, but he appeared to harbor an obsessive hatred for Wallace. He had the Scottish leaders hunt Wallace down; their success in capturing him would allow them to obtain a more lenient punishment from him:

> The King will see how they bear themselves in the business and will show more favor to the man that shall have captured Wallace, by shortening his term of exile, by diminishing the amount of his ransom or of his obligation for trespass, or by otherwise lightening his liabilities. It is further ordained that the Steward, Sir John de Soulis and Sir Ingram de Umfraville shall not have any letters of safe-conduct to come into the power of

the King until Sir William Wallace shall have surrendered to him.[liv]

Despite the tantalizing incentive, none of these men decided to hunt down Wallace. Wallace was an elusive fugitive for two years, as Scotland endured the indignity of all the English constables, sergeants, sheriffs, provosts, tax-gatherers, officials, and soldiers that swarmed through the country, hell-bent on restoring law and order. The rebellious and defiant spirit that the common people had once exhibited had been tamed, leaving behind a docile and submissive populace.

Wallace stood out as a sore thumb in this landscape. The story of his downfall is especially painful to Scottish patriots since he was ultimately betrayed by a fellow Scotsman. The villain in this narrative is Sir John de Menteith,[lv] a knight from one of the most eminent Norman families in Scotland. He had switched sides several times during Scotland's war of independence and had recently returned to Edward's service in September 1303. Edward personally selected him to capture Wallace because Menteith knew Wallace personally. Wallace was an intimate friend and the godfather to Menteith's two sons. This treachery was doubly painful since Menteith had once been highly regarded as a leader of the patriots.

According to Blind Harry, Menteith was reluctant to execute his mission until Edward sent him a personal letter. Menteith then assigned his nephew to join Wallace's band of guerillas so that he could be informed of their movements. When he received news that Wallace had rode out to Robroyston in hopes of meeting Robert Bruce – the man he hoped could restore Scottish independence – Menteith swiftly headed in that direction with sixty of his most loyal men. Wallace was purportedly apprehended at night from the bed he shared with his mistress. Kerly, Wallace's right-hand man, was brutally killed on the spot.

Wallace attempted to fight off Menteith's men with his bare hands (his weapons had been stolen as he slept), but he was hopelessly outnumbered. Blind Harry claims that Menteith then deceived Wallace to get him to surrender, claiming that they were surrounded by a formidable number of English knights and Barons, but that he would be under his protection at Dumbarton Castle. Wallace naively agreed to be bound hand and foot. Upon exiting his tent and seeing Kerly's corpse – and no English army in sight – Wallace realized that he had been tricked.

Menteith was handsomely rewarded with a grant of valuable land, royal favor, and gratuity. In 1306, he was granted the title and earldom of Lennox. Edward had made intricate plans for Wallace to be captured alive so that he could stage a humiliating death that would diminish the power of his reputation. Wallace would not be executed in the Scottish countryside; he would be taken to London for a show trial and the most grotesque manner of death that a medieval mind could imagine. His journey out of the country was made in great secret so as to discourage the possibility that his men or the common people of Scotland might impulsively attempt to free their beloved hero.

Wallace's reputation preceded him in England. Large crowds amassed to watch and jeer at the gigantic young man who had been such a feared enemy in Scotland. The English propaganda machine had painted him as "an ogre of unspeakable depravity who skinned his prisoners alive, burned babies and forced the nuns to dance naked for him." He was also thoroughly decried as a rapist of nuns, a torturer of priests, a mutilator of English soldiers, and arsonists of women and children. Wallace was placed in a heavily guarded house the night he arrived in London, a temporary stop before his trial at Westminster Hall the following morning. His fate may have already been decided by Edward, but the trial was necessary to make a forceful impression on the people of England and Scotland, as well as French sympathizers and the Papacy.

Wallace was swiftly found guilty of sedition, homicide, robbery, arson, sundry, and other crimes. His murder of William de Heselrig, Sheriff of Lanark, was singled out as concrete evidence of his attempt to lead a rebellion against Edward, the "rightful" lord of Scotland. He had also inflicted atrocious cruelties on the English counties of Northumberland, Cumberland, and Westmorland, where he failed to exempt children, women, priests, nuns, churches, and religious relics from violence and destruction. There was no need for witnesses to be examined, for Wallace to be defended by a lawyer, or for the judges to deliberate. Wallace was not even granted the opportunity of defending himself. He did, however, insist on making the crowded hall hear him as he argued that he could not be guilty of treason since he had never pledged his allegiance to Edward.

The punishment that Wallace suffered may seem especially heinous, but it was actually fairly standard procedure for those found guilty of treason during this period. Wallace was stripped naked and drawn by two horses from the Palace of Westminster to the Tower of London, to Aldgate, and through the city to the Elms. As he endured this intentionally long-winded route, the Londoners flung garbage and excrement at him. He was hanged, and then taken down from the gallows before his neck was broken. His genitals were sliced off. He was disemboweled; his intestines were pulled out and burned. The executioner then pulled out his internal organs – the liver, the lungs, etc. – before finally killing Wallace by ripping out his heart. The mob cheered as his head was cut off with a cleaver. The hanging, mutilation, disemboweling, and climactic decapitation was intended to inflict incomparable pain, degradation, and humiliation. His body was cut into four quarters. His head was hung up on the London Bridge, while the four quarters were sent to Newcastle-upon-Tyne, Berwick, Stirling, and St. Johnson "as a warning and a deterrent to all that pass by and behold them."

Conclusion

What remained of William Wallace the man was left to rot in five different locations, denied of the chance to die or be buried in his native Scotland. His flesh would have been pecked at by seagulls and chewed by rats before fully decomposing, leaving behind his bones.[lvi] Eventually, his bones would have been eroded by the weather and disintegrated into oblivion. The Scottish people of Perth or Stirling did nothing to preserve any part of him or to commemorate the man they had once lauded as a national hero. They probably saw his gory execution as a traumatic end of an era. Three weeks after Wallace was no more, the peace settlement of September 1305 was established. The prevailing sentiment might have been that it was better to tolerate Edward's dominion and go on with the rituals of daily life instead of engaging in more arduous years of resistance and battle.

This vision of a more-or-less peaceful submission to England did not come to be. John Balliol would never return to Scotland to regain the crown, but the firm control that Edward desired would be thwarted once again. After Wallace's execution, Robert the Bruce,[lvii] the young Earl of Carrick, emerged as the unexpected new leader of a new and reinvigorated war of independence. Bruce had been a supporter of Wallace and his rebels during the tumultuous years between 1295 and 1304, but he had apparently allied himself with

Edward in recent years. The historical record is unclear if it was Bruce or his followers who had murdered John ("the Red") Comyn in the Franciscan church at Dumfries on February 10, 1306. Comyn was John de Balliol's nephew and Bruce's closest rival as the rightful heir of the Scottish crown. In any case, Bruce's intentions to claim the throne for himself were evident. Six weeks after Comyn's death – and seven months after Wallace's death – Bruce was crowned on March 25 at Scone.

Bruce would succeed where Wallace had failed. From the time he was crowned until Edward's death in 1307, he fought against English rule with the support of the Scottish clergy and his supporters (notably James Douglas and Thomas Randolph, later Earl of Moray). Despite the execution of three of his brothers and the imprisonment of his wife and daughters, Bruce persevered to execute a highly successful guerrilla war against the English army. Bruce suffered two defeats and was eventually forced to go into hiding as a fugitive, but Edward's death and the ineptitude of his fourth son and successor, Edward II,[lviii] allowed him to eventually turn the tables. In 1314, he achieved the historic defeat of a sizable English army at Bannockburn.[lix]

In 1316, Bruce's brother, Edward, was inaugurated as the high king of Ireland, a position he held for only two years before he was killed in battle in 1318. Despite the humiliating defeat at Bannockburn and the Scottish recapture of Berwick, Edward II proved to be as obsessively invested in maintaining his rule over Scotland as his father had been. The Scottish barons, earls, and the entire "community of the realm" eventually turned to diplomatic means to contest his claims. They sent a letter to Pope John XXII[lx] that argued that Robert was the rightful Scottish monarch and that the Scottish people had a right to live under the rule of their own monarchy. In 1324, Robert was recognized by the Papacy as the king of independent Scotland. He renewed the nation's alliance with France with the Treaty of Corbeil,[lxi] which obligated him to attack England if France declared war on it. When Edward II was deposed and replaced by his own son in 1327, peace with England was finally restored. There was one highly important condition: utter renunciation of all English claims to superiority over Scotland.

In the end, Wallace was more powerful in death than he had been in life. He had only enjoyed a short period of fame, power, and glory, punctuated by a crushing defeat and sandwiched between long and painful years in the literal and political wilderness. His willingness to persevere through immense adversity – and the horrifically tragic end he suffered – sealed his legacy as a folk hero. He was a hybrid of King Arthur and Robin Hood; a martyr that became a symbol of the lengths and depths that Scotland was willing to go to free itself from the cursed yoke of English oppression. The movie *Braveheart* included a wholly fictional sexual encounter between Wallace and Princess Isabella (Edward I's daughter-in-law) that could never have occurred, as she only married the Prince of Wales three years after Wallace's death and was a child in France during 1304-05. Their illogical rendezvous nevertheless allows the film to end with a memorable metaphor for the immortality of Wallace's legacy and spirit: Isabella reveals that she is pregnant with Wallace's son to her father-in-law as he suffers from terminal illness, and that his bloodline will not be perpetuated.

Read more biographies from Captivating History

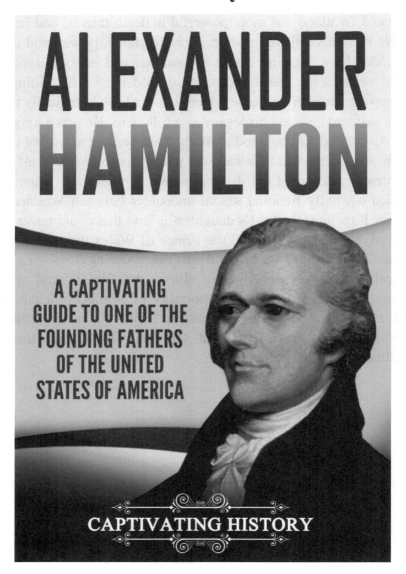

Check out this book!

Click here to check out this book!

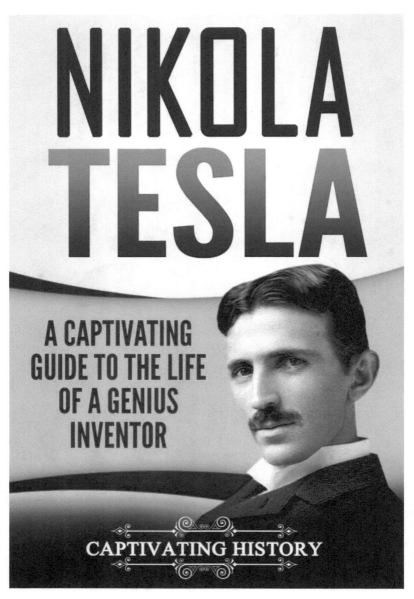

Check out this book!

Check out this book!

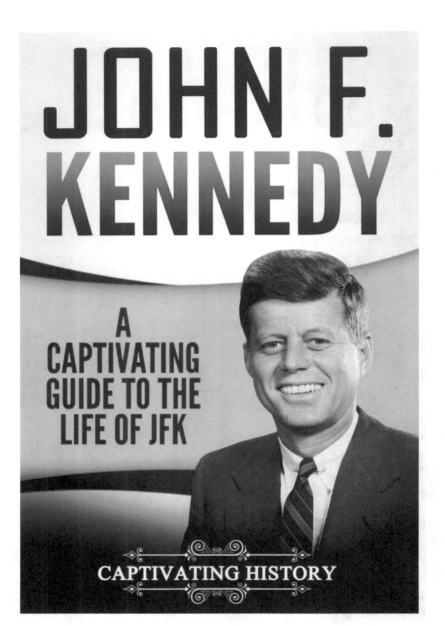

Check out this book!

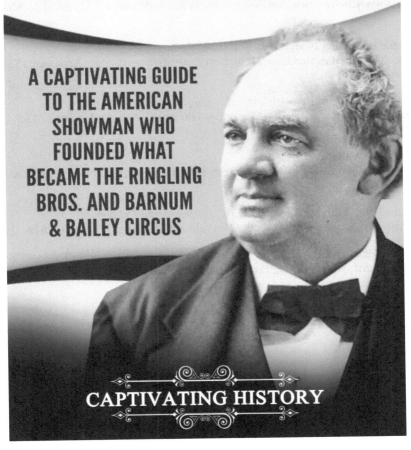

Check out this book!

References

[i] "William Wallace." *Encyclopedia Britannica.*
https://www.britannica.com/biography/William-Wallace. Accessed 15 March 2018.

[ii] "Battle of Stirling Bridge." *Encyclopedia Britannica.*
https://www.britannica.com/event/Battle-of-Stirling-Bridge. Accessed 15 March 2018.

[iii] "Harry the Minstrel: Scottish writer." *Encyclopedia Britannica.*
https://www.britannica.com/biography/Harry-the-Minstrel. Accessed 15 March 2018.

[iv] "William Wallace." *BBC.*
http://www.bbc.co.uk/scotland/history/articles/william_wallace/. Accessed 15 March 2018.

[v] "Braveheart: Film by Gibson [1995]." *Encyclopedia Britannica.*
https://www.britannica.com/topic/Braveheart. Accessed 15 March 2018.

[vi] "Braveheart: dancing peasants, gleaming teeth and a cameo from Fabio." *The Guardian.* **https://www.theguardian.com/film/2008/jul/30/3.** Accessed 15 March 2018.

[vii] "Isabella of France." *Encyclopedia Britannica.*
https://www.britannica.com/biography/Isabella-of-France. Accessed 15 March 2018.

[viii] "William Wallace." *BBC.*
http://www.bbc.co.uk/scotland/history/articles/william_wallace/. Accessed 15 March 2018.

[ix] "Edward I: King of England." *Encyclopedia Britannica.*
https://www.britannica.com/biography/Edward-I-king-of-England. Accessed 15 March 2018.

[x] "Battle of Falkirk." *Encyclopedia Britannica.*
https://www.britannica.com/topic/battle-of-Falkirk. Accessed 15 March 2018.

[xi] "Drawing and quartering." *Encyclopedia Britannica.* https://www.britannica.com/topic/drawing-and-quartering. Accessed 15 March 2018.

[xii] "Robert the Bruce." *Encyclopedia Britannica.* https://www.britannica.com/biography/Robert-the-Bruce. Accessed 15 March 2018.

[xiii] "John Comyn: Scottish leader." *Encyclopedia Britannica.* https://www.britannica.com/biography/John-Comyn. Accessed 15 March 2018.

[xiv] McKay, James. *William Wallace: Brave Heart.* 1995.

[xv] Hamilton, William and Elspeth King. *Blind Harry's Wallace.* 2003.

[xvi] Ibid.

[xvii] "Alexander III: King of Scotland." *Encyclopedia Britannica.* https://www.britannica.com/biography/Alexander-III-king-of-Scotland. Accessed 15 March 2018.

[xviii] Ibid.

[xix] Hamilton, William and Elspeth King. *Blind Harry's Wallace.* 2003.

[xx] "Philip IV: King of France." *Encyclopedia Britannica.* https://www.britannica.com/biography/Philip-IV-king-of-France. Accessed 15 March 2018.

[xxi] "Margaret: Queen of Scotland." *Encyclopedia Britannica.* https://www.britannica.com/biography/Margaret-queen-of-Scotland. Accessed 15 March 2018.

[xxii] "Erik II: King of Norway." *Encyclopedia Britannica.* https://www.britannica.com/biography/Erik-II. Accessed 15 March 2018.

[xxiii] "The Treaty of Birgham." http://www.bbc.co.uk/bitesize/higher/history/warsofindependence/thegreatcause/revision/2/. Accessed 15 March 2018.

[xxiv] "John de Balliol: Scottish magnate." *Encyclopedia Britannica.* https://www.britannica.com/biography/John-de-Balliol. Accessed 15 March 2018.

[xxv] "Robert de Bruce: King of Scotland." *Encyclopedia Britannica.* https://www.britannica.com/biography/Robert-the-Bruce. Accessed 15 March 2018.

xxvi "Henry III: King of England [1207 – 1272]." *Encyclopedia Britannica.* **https://www.britannica.com/biography/Henry-III-king-of-England-1207-1272.** Accessed 15 March 2018.

xxvii Hamilton, William and Elspeth King. *Blind Harry's Wallace.* 2003.

xxviii Rymer, Thomas. *Foedera II.* 1745.

xxix McKay, James. *William Wallace: Brave Heart.* 1995.

xxx Burton, J. Hill. *The History of Scotland.* 1897.

xxxi Bower, Walter and D. E. R. Watt. *Scotichronicon: Books XI and XII.* 1991.

xxxii Hamilton, William and Elspeth King. *Blind Harry's Wallace.* 2003.

xxxiii Murison, A.F. *Famous Scots: Sir William Wallace.* 1898.

xxxiv "Thomas the Rhymer." *Encyclopedia Britannica.* **https://www.britannica.com/biography/Thomas-the-Rhymer.** Accessed 15 March 2018.

xxxv Hamilton, William and Elspeth King. *Blind Harry's Wallace.* 2003.

xxxvi McKay, James. *William Wallace: Brave Heart.* 1995.

xxxvii "Braveheart: Film by Gibson [1995]." *Encyclopedia Britannica.* **https://www.britannica.com/topic/Braveheart.** Accessed 15 March 2018.

xxxviii Rogers, Charles. *The Book of Wallace, vol. II.* 1879.

xxxix"Guerrilla warfare." *Encyclopedia Britannica.* **https://www.britannica.com/topic/guerrilla-warfare.** Accessed 15 March 2018.

xl Murison, A.F. *Famous Scots: Sir William Wallace.* 1898.

xli "John de Warenne, 6th earl of Surrey." *Encyclopedia Britannica.* **https://www.britannica.com/biography/John-de-Warenne-6th-earl-of-Surrey.** Accessed 15 March 2018.

xlii "William Wallace and the Scottish resistance." *BBC.* **http://www.bbc.co.uk/bitesize/higher/history/warsofindependence/williamwallaceandthescottishresistance/revision/2/.** Accessed 15 March 2018.

xliii "Battle of Stirling Bridge." *Encyclopedia Britannica.* **http://www.bbc.co.uk/scotland/history/articles/battle_of_stirling_bridge/.** Accessed 15 March 2018.

xliv Rothwell, H. *Chronicle of Walter of Guisborough.* 1957.

xlv McKay, James. *William Wallace: Brave Heart.* 1995.

xlvi "Battle of Falkirk." *Encyclopedia Britannica.*
https://www.britannica.com/topic/battle-of-Falkirk. Accessed 15 March 2018.

xlvii McKay, James. *William Wallace: Brave Heart.* 1995.

xlviii Rymer, Thomas. *Foedera II.* 1745.

xlix McNair, Ronald. *Robert Bruce, King of Scots.* 1982.

l Bain, Joseph. "Calendar of documents relating to Scotland, preserved in Her Majesty's Public Record Office, London." *Hathi Trust.*
https://catalog.hathitrust.org/Record/000196980/. Accessed 15 March 2018.

li McKay, James. *William Wallace: Brave Heart.* 1995.

lii"Boniface VIII: Pope." *Encyclopedia Britannica.*
https://www.britannica.com/biography/Boniface-VIII. Accessed 15 March 2018.

liii Bower, Walter and D. E. R. Watt. *Scotichronicon: Books XI and XII.* 1991.

liv Murison, A.F. *Famous Scots: Sir William Wallace.* 1898.

lv McKay, James. *William Wallace: Brave Heart.* 1995.

lvi Ibid.

lvii "Robert the Bruce (1274 - 1329)." *BBC.*
http://www.bbc.co.uk/history/historic_figures/bruce_robert_the.shtml. Accessed 15 March 2018.

lviii "Edward II: King of England." *Encyclopedia Britannica.*
https://www.britannica.com/biography/Edward-II-king-of-England. Accessed 15 March 2018.

lix "Battle of Bannockburn." *Encyclopedia Britannica.*
https://www.britannica.com/event/Battle-of-Bannockburn. Accessed 15 March 2018.

lx "John XXII: Pope." *Encyclopedia Britannica.*
https://www.britannica.com/biography/John-XXII. Accessed 15 March 2018.

lxi "Treaty of Corbeil." *Encyclopedia Britannica.*
https://www.britannica.com/topic/Treaty-of-Corbeil. Accessed 15 March 2018.

Free Bonus from Captivating History (Available for a Limited time)

Hi History Lovers!

Now you have a chance to join our exclusive history list so you can get your first history ebook for free as well as discounts and a potential to get more history books for free! Simply visit the link below to join.

Captivatinghistory.com/ebook

Also, make sure to follow us on:

Twitter: @Captivhistory

Facebook: Captivating History:@captivatinghistory

Made in United States
Troutdale, OR
10/22/2023